Scaling the Walls WITHDRAWN

Jonathan Greene

Scaling the Walls

gnomon press

THE AUTHOR would like to thank the editors of the following publications in which many of these poems first appeared: Cid Corman (*Origin* and *The Gist of Origin*, Grossman Publishers), Daryl Hine (*Poetry*), Richard Grossinger (*Io*), Linda Parker (*llama's Allmanac*), David Polk (*The Kentucky Review*), George Quasha (*An Active Anthology*, Sumac Press), David Meltzer (*Tree*), and Thorpe Feidt (*Red Crow*). The following poems first appeared in *Poetry*: 'Where the Blinding Sun' and 'Horror Rations : A Meditation.' 'An Unspoken Complaint' was first published separately by Unicorn Press, Santa Barbara.

Preface

How can I refuse this coin
for my meaningless speech?

The stone endures my song
& what is moved
has no power
in the world.

Fellowship

Rhetoric, what words
for the bony mendicant
coming your way. Sweet
honey breath, tell him
of the sighs a single caesura
can bring:

      Why just yesterday
a couple mated. The source:
one line of verse. No joke,
of course.

      What's that,
spent all night up in a tree?
Come man, change your clothes
& have a drink with me.

The Author

It is his last book.
We see this end
and say *no*. But we know
it is *yes* . . . try to spoil
a line, rearrange pages.

    Language
without voice MEAN
you write striving
upwards in bed. Or later,
think to strive or speak

lost lines we cannot hear.
(*You think we hear, and*
go on sputtering breath.)
We remember the book.
We think 'at least' to his last breath.

Winter : New York City

We never were told
nor was there celebration
leaving childhood's port.
Each return loading more
estrangement into the hold.

Daughter, let me see in you
a fire I can hardly remember,
an innocence that would make
thieves lower their heads
as they pass thru this cold.

An Unspoken Complaint

I know the words.
But what is this
   this voice deep
   within your voice
   which you hide with
   a roughness
   to protect
to protect what?

It's naked anyway.
Though you are not sure I heard it.
And I dare not speak of it.
Selfhood hidden in a hurt.
The once-casual aside
   of a former lover?
A 'sad story' you did not
   plague me with?
I do not know.

Shadows folded within shadows
   & the light
   only for seconds
   of forgetfulness.

  .

We do not speak.
We move on.

We both know something
of what took place.

As if we could never say as much.

Night Shift

1

Flesh is tired
as if it knew
a hundred incarnations
& was still sick of its weight · color · smell.
As if its weight inherited
another world where (*while
in naked sleep & you are close*) the soul is
caught in a factory of night
making bread or steel.

2

There is a taste of steel
in my mouth. I cannot
reach to touch you, tell you
the distraught messages,
the uncommon teachings,
that persist in me.
I leave you to sleep's luxury,
the museum of your clear face
empty of ravages.

Going Through It

Tired of 'being strong'
you want me to take over.
There is equity.
You throw off a burden,
another takes its place.
Just compensation for
pain incurred. Credits &
debits in an other-
worldly account.
Never actually balanced.

The face in the mirror.
The empty bed.
Tired of ambivalence,
tired of always
'being there.'
Empty spaces in
between in-
frequent visits
past midnight.

.

And the perspective.
The open parenthesis.
The lost family
in the heart, a
forsaken enclosure.
'Saving oneself'
for god-knows-what.
Figures of expression.
Literal meanings.

.

How retrace steps down
a forked path back to
its joining. What does
History say about
'repeats'?
The stories recur
in sleep.

.

Holding back & letting go.
The hand a fist.
The hand opening in
invitation.
I face the humiliation
of mistaken invitations.
I reach the clear air.
I fall back.

Parts of the story
go like this:
Knowledge & Experience
were out-of-joint,
running an awkward race
as if one danced
while the other ran
full-steam.
Then the roles
switched.

O, the horses
of instruction
make hard bargains.
Each pulling
a separate direction.
And I
wanting every one of them.

After-knowledge

They called it a dance.
It was no dance.
No simple turning
'round the horizontal
planes of sleep.

Or, as if all songs
were good songs
that said the
right things
(who doesn't
know them).

.

Beyond first meeting,
the uncalled-for
attributes.
Affection's new measure
as the flesh changes
texture in your hand,
in the dream.

The second reading
behind the words
beyond yourself.
Abstract notions
without the
prose commentary
or the speeches
you're used to.

Returned.
Toe stubbed on
the same rock.
Same bed, different
women. Different houses,
the same look. The same
resistance in myself
over space & time.

Taped messages,
atavistic poisons,
that take over
from the here & now,
use my mouth
as carrier.
The next day,
unremembering,
look up at a
hard face
that does.

Mystery then
that we ever
get back to
the brightnesses.

The Excuse

1

She wants
the room perfect.
You enter too soon.

This spoils what's left
of the day, the blouse
opens routinely

every touch a manhandling,
a stale taste *talk*
used to be the 'solution' for.

2

The stranger enters,
sure of himself.
Every instant, each movement,

an expectation of the next.
After sex, before sleep
the late afternoon light

the slight breeze
in the curtain, she scans
the room's chaos with approval.

A Short Visit

Walking in & out of lives.
I thought the chronology always moved forward,
those places left, frozen in their place,
not the actual in front of the eyes–but I hold back
from the return, hold back the knowledge of no return,
touch the Beloved of a former life & ask her
her meaning. *Are you still waiting?*
The thought (naturally) occurs
as the could-have-been can always occur.
We choose other, choose the chronology.

            But I wanted
a way back, wanted to feel my way
along those roads known by heart,
the ones that 'could be driven blindfolded'
& were, in that life.

            Touch that life.
Hold it a sweet minute & hightail it out of there,
the roads left behind for our own purposes labelled
necessary miles not *good* or *bad*.

What are the ways in.
Facts are hopeless.
I could waste night with stories
the measured distances do not know.
Do the words tell (add them up)
what tale, tell me.

Alone Again

It's an emergency,
my heart screaming
down the avenue.

No. It's a slow emergency
with no ambulance, no doctor,
no hospital & charts.

This is among the mortal things
whose torture comes, stays, passes
unnoticed by others.

Raise your hand in the loneliness.
Comparative Pain an impossible course
in the curriculum –

everyone never letting
anyone else speak.

Shapes as Remonstrances to the Past

Are they the spare parts
or essential, limbs or torso,
which atrophy when you're gone,
which rest in that automobile graveyard
of haphazard memories.

But it's past that now. Passed out of a present
into a mandala whose center is a negative space
that sucks in the color around it until the forms
are empty, black & white, denuded,
where the richness had been.

This black-on-white also – one of its forms.

Wall-talking

There is a conversation
cut in half
not like a cake
but as a limb
lost in a machine

There is a lost opportunity
& at the end of
each sentence,
from habit, I ask
the emptiness

do you hear me,
do you know what I mean?

Sleepless in Montana

Women, they have been teachers,
have been spirits of the dream,
a warmth the memory seeks
for shelter.

       Endless whirlpool
sucked into, the anatomy
of what I've lost
comes back now:

I lie awake
trying to believe
your loveliness is
part of my story.

Self-mourning

All the broken relics are easy to take,
all the missing books, the table with
three legs. But these as portions of
a dream: *fire of fierce vision, verse
to storm a deaf age* – this burnt into
my life an empty space to cry out from.
I did not want to cry out only concealed
fragments, confirmations of loss.

You had left.
How long was it
I hadn't noticed.

In My Weakness I Remember

I

Those who have carried away from love its aftertaste,
who can be generous in their leave-taking. Those
who have been left alone with the darkness of cold walls,
empty, suicidal. I have been both & did not choose either.

You who approach me now do not see this history in my face,
the outward signs. Instead puzzlement follows when, after
your hands have eased the age's weariness from me, I shiver
at your touch & hold back as if you, who proffer gifts,
were rapist & thief.

2

I am not sure I can remember all the narrative
that has brought me here. I am not sure
you are interested. My nerves need recoding &
the teacher must be patient. The self-pity
is ending. Other weaknesses are coming
to take its place. As if I were advertising,
to you or myself, for guard duty in front
of a burnt-out shrine.

And the necessities so tedious, so unlikely
either of us can purify these desires
into everyday unasked-for bounty.

Dance of the Opposites

The flexibility, say, of a hundred boxers
crowding a ring which is the body they war in,
the body the world never sees.

Bare-fisted anger, say, that even Love at times portrays.
But each boxer so agile he can always just escape
each punch thrown, a balance of the needed information
that steps through a door the exact moment an opening
occurs.

Theory in despair throws more men in the ring,
in exasperation later withdraws almost all in hopes
that the few left might grow in strength and
one argument triumph in an ecstasy of self-love
& righteousness.

In the body the world never sees, they all embrace
& separate, separate & embrace at the edge of sleep,
unknown forces of the day.

Morning Misgivings

Early Sunday ratiocination where each second
reaches its own conclusion. This 'sounds' right
and I know it's right, but something in my blood
refuses this, a chemical that goes down fighting,
that never lets me be in present tense, keeps *now*
waiting in bad neighborhoods 'til it's ready for
plush times.

Better to be detached & like a detective examine
table tops for the deciduous leftovers from
past seasons, what clothes have become attached
to chairs like lichen, as if these were mirrors
of inner shape or shapelessness.

As if proof were needed in such detail—so deaf
I could not hear the world singing matins at
daybreak.

of fortune
reath
ver them again
slowly so I can understand
in time with my slow understanding
which dwells for months
on the same small perception
turning it over & over
in my mind
'til the poem is written.

And when it is written
I relax & go to sleep
only to wake to pronouncements
of the future
she has to tell me now
& can't wait & *you will have time enough
later for sleep*—thus through
the emptiness there are many movements
to hide the emptiness—
but finally I lie awake without understanding
& want to know & cry out from the cold
why the years have subtracted knowledge
& left me to face this end
without knowing if this is
the methodology
of a slow dying.

The Continuities

The continuities seem to end,
the narrative cord scissored,
the beads of a necklace
on the floor in hopeless
scramble, & the mind awakened
by visions of a former life.

Haunted, no ladder, the failed
poems never transforming
into the *clear taut line*.
This is the necessary sleep,
the failure of a single intent
willing the world to its shape.

A Solace

At despair's
absolute zero
or right before that
he puts the needle
on a certain worn groove
of the Brandenburg
& nears a gentle field
to let the comparison
speak for his waste
& yet be a fuzzy consolation
for the race.

Abstract Poem : The Details Are Yours

Locked tight
in a fantasy.

Then came an absurd irony.
An idea. An event. A crowbar
of light with too much meaning.

Too many years the same,
& now the skull splintered
on what his life had been for.

Eating Next to Businessmen

Flushed red
from drink
they divide & conquer.

We remember for them
what's under this din
of false-boisterous times.

We can turn off the sound
& a charade appears with
clear meanings. And then

we can still their movements:
all suffering, all sentient
beings, all needing care.

A Small Puddle

A small puddle of phlegm in all this sunlight,
a corruption in all this mindless passivity.
Vacated image.

           Artaud studied the faceless,
unformed flesh. I too. *Eat my heart out,*
living amongst, unrecognized.

               A voice here
that wants to be a huckster selling that pool
to the backyards of America, writing a poem
full of broken bottles, bad breath
& a sweat that comforts tired muscles,
that wants to make speeches saying:
here's your forgotten shadow,
this toothless bum the spin-off,
the asset you forgot to claim.

Poem the Limnologist Overlooked

Sublet my body
to the Lady of Lead.
She said: *I want*
to fly. On acid
there is a certain
danger.

Thinking I could help, forgot her nature.
She carried me down to pondbottom
in an embrace that began with need,
ended with languor.

Some summer nights,
beyond the shadow
of the trees,
I see the stars
touch surface
& come no deeper.

The Cure

The eyes blur.
The pain is in my head,
in my left chest,
the trouble is in
our age or youth
or wanting to be
elsewhere
with a teacher
to tell us what to do,
a doctor to calm us,
a woman to take
our fantasies away.

The trouble is in
the pain we love,
the hurt we cause others
because they love their own.

The definitions hurt
not saying enough,
give too little
understanding,
hold back
the complete saying.

Or take us away
with inner talking,
talking endlessly,
running on like this
after lost aims
& slights from fate,
our neighbors.

Abulia, the doctor
states, typical
of our age,
a pill every
3 hrs. of not
knowing who you
are
      a digestive
after every meal
listening to the news,
watching it in colors.

Soon you'll be
asleep like the rest
but without the anxiety,
but with shadows of
shadows of anxiety,
but with lost concern
lost in shadows
of self hood,
similacra
crystallized
in vagueness.

The blurred lines
in the air of our speech
not worth the telling
on television
every night
telling us
that.

Inferno without System

Some talk on the steps at night. A need. A possibility.
Then sex across the boundaries of marriage, unknowing
prelude to six years of tenuous connections.

The thread running deep in her, in him – an uncomfortable
indulgence. With a cold eye, a list of: attempted suicide,
miscarriage, abortion. With another eye, warmth hard to
come by after empty days.

After the abortion, the nurse sadistically tells her
the gender. But the fetus is partial, the pain continues.
At home, in the bathroom, she gives birth to a leg –
small, perfect.

As if an image created for an unnatural joining,
it announces banishment.

Where Are the Fine Lines

Where are the fine lines?
We can't lay it down so.
Let the figure have some reign
& he destroys the well-knit page,
spills over the carefully drawn borders
into another land: strange to himself
to wander there.

                Lost in a wood.
This is a fiction we imagine. Death
in the movies, on television, in the
imagination of a dying man. These borders
are no longer tangible. That a fiction we imagine
is real, that a man dying alone in a wood might
experience it less. Levels & layers removed from
what they were, a forsaken simplicity.

                          I *am* lost.
This is literal & exact. The woods are traditional,
optional, no longer to the point.

The Room

for John Wieners

This room, walls I'd rather not have.
This suffering – the same.
That I have gloried here is not the point.
At the bottom of a pit, as if words
were a ladder out. Given a few hours
the walls are substantial again.
Letters sink here – all 'after the fact'
or for some reason do not reach in.
Do they think these walls shed light
& words a greater light adding to a sum total.
Hardly ever light & never added.

In this room I wait.
Beyond touch, or where touch
is a hotel of former lovers
& who is there now I only think I know.
In the bone's old history: *every yearning*
is cause for new yearning & new reticence.
I spend myself, though the cost is never as high
as in the dream, the heroic expense account
not called for, only desired.

How many are we: ghosts escaping shadows
that threaten to appear, threaten death
– as we mean them to – for the love
that does not come.

Interview

What happened here? Body splayed out before the
casual customer. Give them the handle of facts,
of dates, some quotes out of context (to justify
the fuss), photographs in characteristic settings,
and a few secrets for revelation.

*No more photographs, no more statements for the press.
The style of one in the foreground against a background
of events, a quick blur painted for history. The eye of
the camera is set on too slow a speed, your system
slower still. What you missed burns like phosphorous.*

Horror Rations : A Meditation

To keep our humanity we turn off the news.
To keep healthy we don't read newspapers.
Or do so once a month. Or twice a year. That's enough.
Otherwise we become rigid, lose our ability to react,
show our wisdom to this folly in pat phrases,
surface shelters. You know this is the truth.

It's always all there plain to see.
A pile of dead by the roadside: enemy dead.
Slung on top of a truck: 'our' dead. No.
The dead have no country. But, how often should
we watch. Should we forget to walk the clean cold air
of winter. Sit inside, tear all violence out of self,
calm one's self. Save one's own skin, care those ways
& means. Show the face of peace & strength to the
face of lies, the men of the Lie. Do you cry at the
news story, the monotone of facts. Is this a measure.
It is and you want to deny it. You grow weary, your
attention no longer focuses. They have won.

Where the Blinding Sun

Where the blinding Sun burns, they tell stories of the Sun.
They sit in the shade of night & tell the stories before
sleep.

Each of us in the shade of a story holds & hides what blinds
us. It binds us. Close as the hide that covers us.

To sleep in a story, he said. Sun was too much & I went in.
Come out again, she said. Don't stop & look for hidden meanings
or the story changes. Don't stare or there is a different one
telling it.

Each telling, each breath, tells. Tolls the moment. Lost threads
make a graveyard. What gets lost & what found. *First & last
questions are first to be forgotten,* said the King. *Was it
King Sun? Son of a shade?* the little boy wondered.

Determine these things. Images the whores of impulse. We
pay for it. *Mlle. Word-play how much do you cost?* leading
dismembered parts through your labyrinth. *In truth,* cried
the toll-master, *too many personages to get the story
straight.* Too many lost threads, Sleep tells us.

Insidious

My pen
finds the despair
I left behind.

I'll throw it away
to placate Optimism,
who keeps me smiling.

Then, Despair will come
looking for the voice
I knew myself by.

It will hand me a new pen
with an innocent look.
I'll take it sheepishly.

A few bad lines that won't do
will once again make me
its functionary

scraping & bowing
small-step-shuffle
backwards out the door.

City Constitutional

Reflexes jump.
I wasn't warned.
The sound of November leaves
each a murderer.
What we don't trust
anymore.
In sleep each night
the sirens
the tires' screech
heard turning on
to the avenue.
We turn
& the wind through
the skyscrapers
a low howl or hum
like an over-announced cortège
coming for us.

Implacable

Imported from catalogues
the houses are coming,
marching on the farmlands.

Each night, how sweetly
the cars come home, nudge gently
into their moorings

wake the house up, put it to sleep.
Houses like innocent daughters
whose mothers died in childbirth.

Adversary Notions

This poem here,
trying to be gentle,
crushed that seedling.
And that painting,
trying to hold
time still, lost
its chance to
be here. This novel
being clever, a
memory of small
exactitudes, a
Shiva octopus with
microscopes for fingertips,
forgets events take place
with less clarity.

Broken mirrors,
imaginary realms,
for worlds
you did not want
to touch, whose
fiery body—a refused
gift, a lost meaning.

A Methodology

Body says: *sleep*.
Mind moving: there's
a storm of trivia
& plots to fame
crowding this space.

And yesterday
we talked of will
& how we keep
meaning to remember
the larger aims.

And today an abstract
lack of warmth
in the world
spells out a smaller life
for everyone.

Mind settles:
comfort in our
great undiscovered
nothingness, *grain of sand*
or *lost in the stars*.

Body: gets typical
gut reaction to that!
all extremities waver.
Mind: dreams out loud
then to itself (asleep).

Moonless Night

Symptoms of vertigo in the toes and fingertips.
One remembers remembering the lost dream that
hangs there just out of reach, as if I were
the one asleep at the foot of a Jacob's ladder
that rested in the skull, entire. As if it
would have brought some light if it could.

This is probably another lie that puts me to
sleep in the morning, that wakes me at night
and tells me what I don't know and now forget.
Knowingly. *Probably*. Also.

Recognitions Beyond

I see the possibility
I deny. The surroundings
not to the point. Anywhere
– that possibility. An oblique
tangent to the everyday.
(*Given the place to stand*,
Archimedes said. . .)

. . . to start with total
recognition of the moment.
Proceed to the inner by
the skin of our assumed flesh.
In the beginning: 'I never
knew before' as answer.
At the end: hand-over-mouth
yes, touch the matter.

A Distance

Where are the words.
The old man sits smoking his pipe,
will answer but will not proffer
talk of the hour or day.
Across the table the young
rush to speak. For the youngest,
naming of things in a book:
eyes – object in the book – object in the world – the word.
This grasp, another departure, towards the naming
that fogs a thing over, distorts the object,
holds no weight. A distance.

The desire, the old man
touching grand-daughter's cheek,
her impatient running away,
unknowingly towards this distance.
His light of 'certain' days make this day.
The commonplace no longer a book to write from,
always it is raise to the n'th power,
not show forth the power there.
Always the heroic gesture,
that turns upon itself,
creates its own distance.

We have lost the days.
This is a story recurs each day.
Forgotten 'til heard once more.
Or seen in the face of an old man
silent at day's close: words
are losses to him
who distills pure light.

Chosen

In winter's cold
every house a sanctuary,
every car & truck
an inviolate capsule of light
wending its way home.

Snow drinks up their noise
and sounds of the other seasons.
Sitting in the cold dark
of the outhouse
a breath swallows

the beautiful pill of
a new life.
Body accepts.
Changed. Rooted.
Later realized:

mind played no part.

Chair Thoughts

As she tears the thread
with her teeth,
a tamed violence in the eyes,
the head tilted to the side,
   she looks up.

Patching old clothes
like getting caught
in underbrush.

But when you finished
knitting that sweater
(a way the hands
transcended
nervous boredom)
there was a purity
with that creation,
a triumph,
         the impatience gone
as the last piece
was bound off.

A clear stream, perhaps,
in a mountain meadow.

When these actions,
these places,
remember each other
there could be
an acceptance

makes the mind smile.

Learning from Objects

The cupboard in all humility
hid things away, not as we do
with the pretense that the secrets
are the true implements of our
Being the world will never
judge us by.

This plate herein with no name,
anyone can eat from it. This
good frying pan that will
outlast us, cook a thousand eggs.
And tea cups to pour mellowness
down us and our failure
to conserve that warmth.

If only we could find
the right things to say
with the ease of making dinner
& bring the day to its close.

Depth Comprehension

You must understand: emerald & dark green the water.
Understand a sudden space opening in time.

Space into which one single dandelion pappus skims
the water, takes off higher in a slight updraft,
goes toward land as if it knew the currents of air
& its intelligence is very great.

Understand this creates a space instrumented away
from time. Breathless. Some very small breath,
less than a child's, does this.

You must know this. And know how these things get
lost & dull ambitions (with machinations as cruel
as that breath was sweet) take such a seeing away
& hand us false burdens to love.

To Keep the Earth Alive

These light years
this light has travelled
to find this hand
reaching for your hand
to find the fire
there.

There is a space
between us, very close,
but before touch.
Touch is its
aftermath.

This is reported back
to the aether
& once again
the end is
forestalled.

Scaling the Walls

It's an orphaned home,
not the original.

Isn't it always like this!

Kicked out of childhood,
rudely. Later, daydreams
anchored in their impossibility
& our need.

    Lost in the snow
the high drifts change
familiar ground.

And if the familiar can
grow strange, one
learns to love
the new dark,
the new light.

.

At night
hands come
as if our flesh
were gloves waiting
for these hands to enter,
lead us past our knowing.

For first we gave will
more tether
& then it's a kite
we lose the string of
in the next meadow.

In the morning
it comes back
'sense of ourselves'
a sharp eye
on the memory of night
(denial & unbelief).

.

Sweet day when
night will stay
constant brother
in the shadows
(in the underside
of your touch,
undertow of
eye-depth,
and the peace
of having place
there).

ds I'd like sent up,
allows. Like the anxious ones
: poem–send them up first.
Then those ove. .. ere buying surfaces
for the dust to nap on–those next.
Then the show-offs, insecurity so hidden
they wear 500 masks–I want to see
truckloads of their heads moving down
the highway

        . . . all these hundreds
& more, behead them that crowd my head,
spring up again, eternal weeds that
embrace me, shadow the earth.

But what of those few milling about,
muttering like workers before a strike,
who tell me I love the rhetoric of despair?

Spare them for my better self to hear.

Chögyam Trungpa Answers a Disciple

His answer – beyond the furthest reach
of a boomerang. He who threw it, his fingers
could but graze the returning curve.

*One thousand copies of this book have been
composed & printed by Heritage Printers, Inc.,
in Monotype Bembo for gnomon press, Post Office
Box 1796, Lexington, Kentucky, 40501. Of which
125 copies have been bound by hand, signed &
numbered by the author. Cover illustration
is from a photograph by Anne Frye.*